mighty machines

RACING MACHINES

Written by
James Pickering

Illustrated by
Colin Howard

This is a Parragon Book
First published in 2001

Parragon
Queen Street House
4 Queen Street
Bath BA1 1HE, UK

Copyright © Parragon 2001

Produced by

David West 🏃 Children's Books
7 Princeton Court
55 Felsham Road
Putney
London SW15 1AZ

All rights reserved. No part of this publication
may be reproduced, stored in a retrieval system,
or transmitted by any means, electronic,
mechanical, photocopying, recording or
otherwise, without the prior permission of the
copyright holder.

British Library Cataloguing-in-Publication Data

A catalogue record for this book is available from
the British Library.

ISBN 0-75254-675-9

Printed in U.A.E

Designer
David West
Illustrator
Colin Howard
(SGA)
Cartoonist
Peter Wilks
(SGA)
Consultant
Steve Parker

CONTENTS

4 Who raced a horse and carriage in a train?

5 Who first raced in cars?

6 Who used a rocket to go faster than 1000 kph?

6 Who put a rocket on a bike?

7 Who went faster than the speed of sound in a car?

8 Which cars race to a formula?

9 What's an Indycar?

9 Which cars race for 24 hours?

10 When is a saloon car not a saloon car?

10 What is stock car racing?

11 Who races through dirt and ice?

12 Who waves a chequered flag?

12 Who wears fireproof underwear?

? Who raced a horse and carriage in a train?

In 1825, George Stephenson raced his engine *Locomotion* against a team of horses, and won. For the first time ever, he showed that a mechanical vehicle could travel more quickly than a horse-drawn carriage.

Locomotion

Amazing! Racing machines have been around for a very long time. The Romans used to race horse-drawn chariots more than 2000 years ago. Their chariots had two wheels which were connected by a wooden axle. It must have been a bumpy ride. The drivers used to stand up to drive, for balance. The more horses, the faster the chariot went.

Is it true?
In 1897, a cyclist beat a motorbike in a race.

Yes. A man called W.J. Stocks pedalled over 43 kilometres on his bicycle in one hour, and beat a motorbike by 270 metres. The rider of the motorbike was not happy. He said that the crowd was too noisy and had put him off!

Early motor race, France 1902

? Who first raced in cars?

The first ever race was in 1894 between Paris and Rouen in France. The Count de Dion won in a steam powered car, which could only manage 18 kph. Early motor races showed people that cars were as fast and reliable as horses.

Who used a rocket to go faster than 1000 kph?

In 1970, American Gary Gabelich drove his rocket powered car, *The Blue Flame*, at 1,016 kph through the Bonneville Salt Flats, and it's still the world's fastest rocket car. When he wasn't breaking records, Gary also raced dragsters and worked as a test astronaut.

Who put a rocket on a bike?

Richard 'Rocketman' Brown started building *The Challenger* in 1996. It has three rocket engines, which produce about 12,200 horsepower per tonne, taking it to 530 kph!

Challenger

Rocket powered car

7

Is it true?
Some cars need parachutes.

Yes. Some cars are so fast that brakes alone aren't powerful enough to stop them. Parachutes drag these cars back to lower speeds when they're travelling very quickly. *Thrust SSC* has four parachutes to bring it back below the sound barrier.

Who went faster than the speed of sound in a car?

Briton Andy Green set a world record in 1997, when he drove the jet-powered *Thrust SSC* at 1,227.985 kph through the Nevada desert.

Thrust SSC

Amazing! As early as 1904, some cars could travel at more than 160 kph! Louis Rigolly was the first person to reach this speed in his enormous 100 horsepower Gobron-Brillié car, during the July Speed Trials in Ostend, Belgium. Luckily he didn't crash. Seatbelts hadn't been invented, and Rigolly only wore a cloth cap to protect his head!

Gobron-Brillié

Which cars race to a formula?

There are very strict formulas or rules about how racing cars are built. Formula One cars' size, shape and petrol tank are all governed by rules, so that every race is fair.

Amazing! Although go-carts are much smaller than other racing cars, they can reach speeds of up to 250 kph! Carting is very popular among young drivers, and many Formula One stars, like Michael Schumacher, used to race carts.

Ferrari formula one racing cars

Is it true?
Modern racing cars have wings.

Yes. They are at the front and back of the car. A racing car's wings are carefully designed to stop the car from taking off. As air passes over the wing, it pulls the car down on to the track. This gives the driver better control and roadholding.

What's an Indycar?

Indycar racing takes place at the Indianapolis Motor Speedway in America. They have powerful engines and huge fins.

Indycar

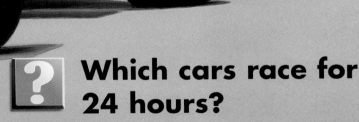

Which cars race for 24 hours?

Sports cars race around the Le Mans circuit in France for 24 hours. Two or three drivers take turns at the wheel to drive the car as far as possible.

Le Mans sports car

9

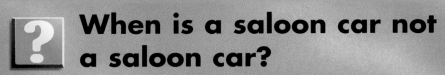

❓ When is a saloon car not a saloon car?

When it's competing in the saloon car championships. The cars in these races look like the family cars you might see on the road, but underneath their bodywork is a specially built, very fast racer.

Saloon cars

Amazing! Modern saloon racers lift themselves into the air on tall stilts! Like all racing cars, saloon cars have to make regular pit stops during races. Repairs, adjustments and tyre changes need to be made as quickly as possible. These stilts save the mechanics from having to crawl under the car.

❓ What is stock car racing?

Stock car racing is organised by the National Association for Stock Car Auto Racing in America. Stock cars look quite like ordinary road cars, but they have much more powerful engines and extra safety features.

Stock cars

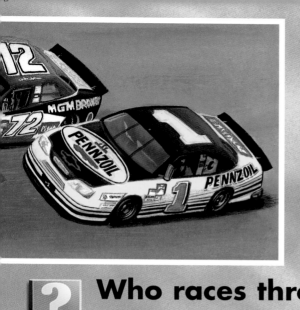

No. The body shell of a stock car is in one piece. This reduces the weight of the car and improves safety. There's no glass on the driver's side either, so he or she has to climb in and out of the car through the empty window!

Who races through dirt and ice?

Rally cars are built to compete in races on muddy tracks, across country and even through snow. In such slippery conditions, accidents can happen, and often do!

Rally car

11

? Who waves a chequered flag?

Race officials aren't allowed to talk with drivers during a race, so they communicate with flags. Different flags warn of danger, problems, or may order a driver off the track. The chequered flag is waved in front of the winning car.

End of race

Danger

Mechanical problems

All clear

The race has been stopped

? Who wears fireproof underwear?

Underneath their overalls, racing drivers must wear fire-resistant 'Nomex' underwear, made up of a long sleeved vest, full length pants, socks and a balaclava. These protect the driver against a blaze of 700° C for twelve seconds.

Amazing! In dry conditions, bald tyres provide better grip than tyres with grooves. In the rain, cars switch to tyres with deep slots, to disperse as much water as possible and prevent skids. Each tyre can disperse 26 litres of water from the road per second!

Is it true?
Racing cars could race across the ceiling.

Yes. The air pressure pushing a speeding racing car on to the track is so great that they could race upside down.

13

Unsportsman-like behaviour

Slippery track

Designated car must stop at pits

A driver wants to overtake

Slow vehicle on track

? **Who works in the pit?**

About 20 mechanics work in the pits, where they make quick repairs and adjustments during a race. They can change a wheel in under five seconds!

Pit crew

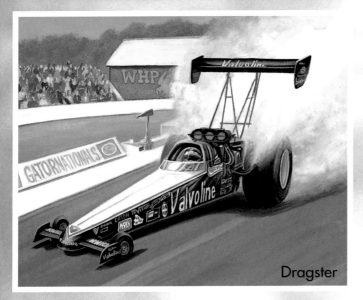
Dragster

Amazing!
Dangerous things can happen at 480 kph. A blowover is when the front wheels lift off the ground and the whole car flips over backwards! Modern dragsters have a safety device called a wheelie bar, which keeps the car on solid ground.

? Which cars race in a straight line?

Dragsters are specially built racers, which look and perform like nothing you would ever see on the road. A drag race is a noisy hurtle down a straight 400 metre track, at around 520 kph! Dragsters are designed with only one thing in mind – acceleration.

Pro Stock drag bike

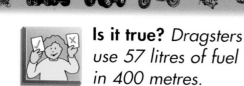

Is it true? *Dragsters use 57 litres of fuel in 400 metres.*

Yes. Dragsters are thirsty beasts! Over 400 metres, a dragster can use the same amount of fuel that a modern family car might burn on a 600 kilometre journey.

What is a funny car?

Funny cars are bizarre looking versions of family cars, which take part in some drag races. The bodywork is stretched out of shape, to fit over a huge supercharged engine and chassis. They're decorated with bright colours and patterns.

Funny car

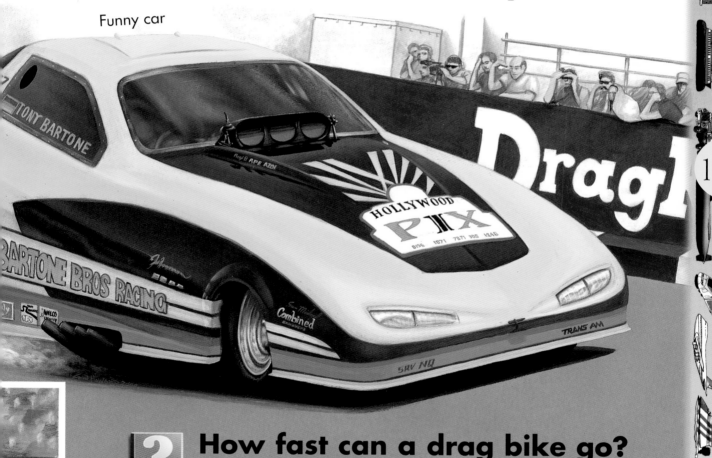

How fast can a drag bike go?

Pro Stock drag bikes are two wheeled dragsters, or four wheelers, if you count their two rear stabilisers, which help to control them at high speeds. Drag bike ace John Mafaro reached 284.85 kph in 1991!

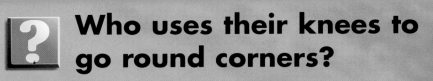

❓ Who uses their knees to go round corners?

Riders in motorbike Grands Prix take corners very quickly by leaning sharply into bends, scraping their knee against the track. This is called the 'knee down' position. For protection, they have tough nylon knee pads sewn into their leathers.

Sidecar racing bikes

❓ Which motorbike racers have three wheels?

Sidecar racing bikes have three wheels. The sidecar isn't powered, but the second rider provides vital balance. On corners, the sidecar rider leans out, for extra roadholding, and the driver hardly has to reduce speed.

16

Amazing! Some bikes have tyres with metal spikes sticking from them, for riding on ice. The spikes pierce the icy surface and stop the bike from skidding. Without them, both bike and rider would go flying!

Knee down position

Is it true?
Motorbike races last only one hour.

No. Different races have different lengths. The famous Le Mans race in France, for example, lasts for an exhausting 24 hours, while speedway races are often run over just four laps (1200 metres) and last for about a minute!

Which motorbikes don't have brakes?

Speedway racing bikes don't have brakes. Instead, the bike slows to an almost instant halt, as soon as the throttle is released. Riders wear extra sturdy steel boots, which they grind into the dirt, to bring the bike to a final standstill.

Speedway racing bikes

Who races across the Sahara?

Competitors in the Paris-Dakar rally set off from the French capital and race for 20 days, until they reach the capital of Senegal, West Africa. Cars have to withstand extremes of temperature, and the rigours of travelling through the dust and sand of the Sahara desert.

Amazing! In trials competitions, high speeds are not allowed! Trials riders jump over obstacles, with penalties for putting a foot on the ground. They mustn't go faster than 24 kph.

Rally carts

What are rally carts?

Rally carts are speedy four wheeled, outdoor go-carts, designed for cross-country racing. They have wide tyres to cope with bumpy ground, powerful engines, and roll-cages, in case of a tumble!

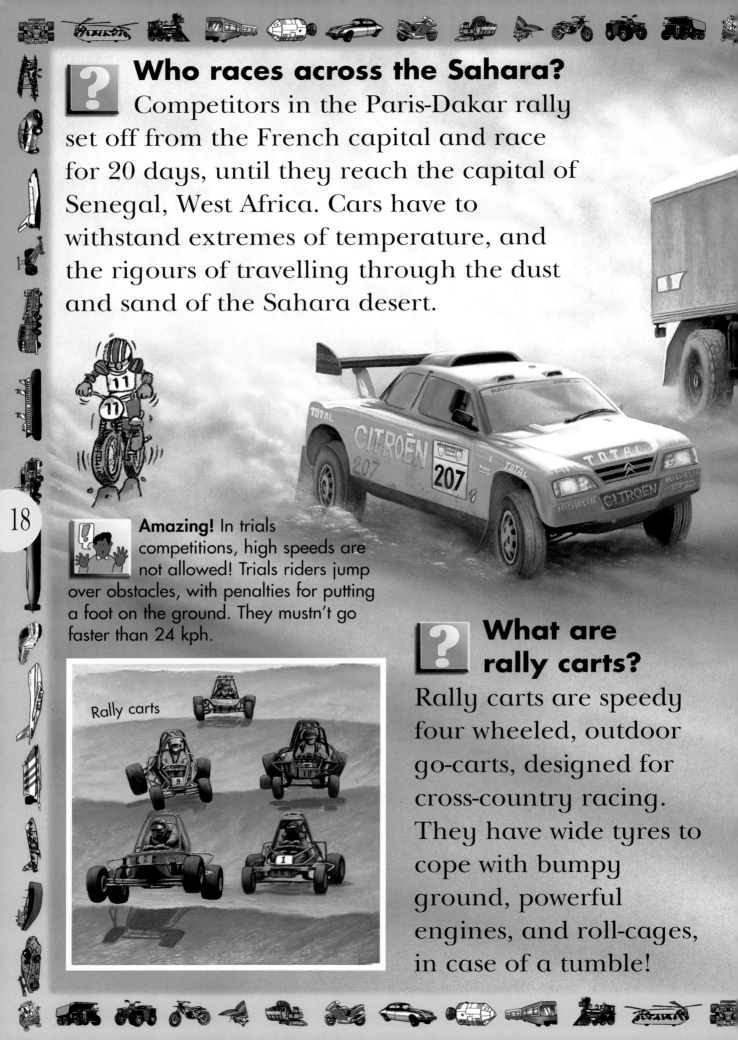

Paris-Dakar rally

Is it true?
Some bikes have three wheels.

Yes. Many ATVs (All Terrain Vehicles) have three wheels. They can be raced or used on farms for getting around safely and quickly. Quad bikes have four wheels, with thick tyres and improved suspension.

? Which racecourse has jumps?

There are plenty of jumps and bumps on cross-country motorbike scrambles or moto cross. Riders roar across the toughest terrain there is, through muddy woods, fields and even snow!

Moto cross

? Who raced hotrods along the street?

There used to be a dangerous trend in America for racing at night through the streets in souped-up road cars, nicknamed 'hotrods'. The official sport of hotrod racing was founded to put an end to racing on the road.

Hotrods

Monte Carlo Grand Prix

Is it true?
Racing cars are not allowed to race in cities any more.

No. Several Grands Prix are still run on public roads. The event at Monte Carlo has been held on almost exactly the same circuit since 1929. The Australian Grand Prix in Melbourne is another example. The streets are cleared of public traffic in advance and crash barriers are set up. Dozens of classic car rallies also run from town to town.

? What were café racers?

Café racers were specially modified bikes, which were raced to and from roadside cafés. This craze started in England in the 1960s. Not surprisingly, café racing on public roads is against the law!

? Who wears a yellow shirt if he's winning?

The overall leader in the exhausting Tour de France bicycle race wears a bright yellow shirt. Recently some stages of the race have been run in southern England, Spain and Belgium, as well as France.

Amazing! In July 1924, Ernest Eldridge broke the World Land Speed Record on a French public road. He was driving a specially built 1907 Fiat called *Mephistopheles* and reached 234 kph!

Mephistopheles

21

Which race needs sunshine?

There's a race every year in Australia for sunshine, or solar-powered, cars. *The Sunraycer* is one contender, with dozens of solar cells across its bodywork. These recharge its batteries and power the electric motor. *Sunraycer* crossed the country at an average speed of 40 kph.

Is it true?
Violent Violet *broke the electric speed record.*

Yes. Superbike *Violent Violet* managed a speed of 166 kph, to become the world's fastest electrically powered motorbike. *Violet* has massive tubes, which direct cooling air to her powerful motor, and a heavy powerpack at the rear.

Violent Violet

The Belgian Bullet

Amazing! In 1899, one electric car could easily outperform any petrol-driven vehicle. Belgian Camille Jenatchy invented a magnetic motor and put it in a torpedo-shaped car, nicknamed *The Belgian Bullet*. The car took him to a speedy 105 kph!

Which cars don't need petrol?

Electric and solar powered cars don't use petrol. Since the 19th century, people have built cars which don't burn liquid fuel. Unfortunately, they can be less reliable and slower than petrol driven vehicles.

Electric car

How fast can a Sinclair C5 go?

In 1996, Adam Harper attempted to reach 240 kph, and break the British electric car land speed record, in *Alien*, a modified, electric Sinclair C5.

Alien

❓ Where do you come first if you are last?

A demolition derby is not so much a race as a test of strength. Modified road cars deliberately smash into one another, and the winner is the last car to keep moving. It's a dangerous sport, and drivers are protected by harnesses and safety cages.

Amazing! Some tractors are powered by aircraft engines! *Tractor Tuggers* have to drag a sledge weighing a hefty 100 tonnes, for 100 metres along a dirt track.

Tractor Tugger

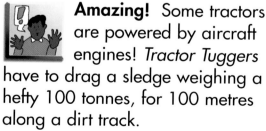

Gravity Formula One

? Which racing cars have no engines?

Gravity Formula One cars are downhill racers, which have no engines, just a steering lever and a small brake. Drivers skid them down steep mountain roads at speeds of around 100 kph!

 Is it true?
People race lawnmowers.

Yes. Some people really do take their lawnmowers racing. It's cheaper than Formula One, and it keeps the grass down as well. It just goes to show that if it's got wheels, someone out there will race it!

Demolition derby

25

? Are there races for trucks?

Yes. Specially tuned trucks compete on racetracks. They look like ordinary trucks on the road, but they're a lot faster. Some even have jet engines, reaching speeds of over 605 kph!

Racing trucks

? Who wears a crash helmet at sea?

Powerboat drivers have to wear crash helmets. Powerboats are made from tough aluminium and each crew member is attached to a cord which cuts the engine if they fall out. These boats can reach 220 kph (120 knots)!

Amazing! Powerboats can take off. At high speed, air can become trapped beneath them, lifting the boat above the water, with disastrous results.

Powerboat

? Who's the fastest man on water?

Kenneth Warby managed an official speed of 511 kph (276 knots) in his hydroplane *Spirit of Australia* in 1978, on Blowering Dam in Australia.

Hydroplane

❓ Which boats use water jets?

Jet boats and jet skis use water jets to power them. In the same way that the jet engine of an aircraft forces hot gas backwards, sending the plane forwards, a water jet pushes pressurised water backwards, driving the boat forwards. Bumpy but great fun!

Jet ski

Is it true?
Some racing boats are powered by fans.

Yes. Hovercraft are powered by fan-like propellers, mounted high in the air, so they can travel over land as well as water. Underwater propellers would get clogged with weeds in swampy rivers.

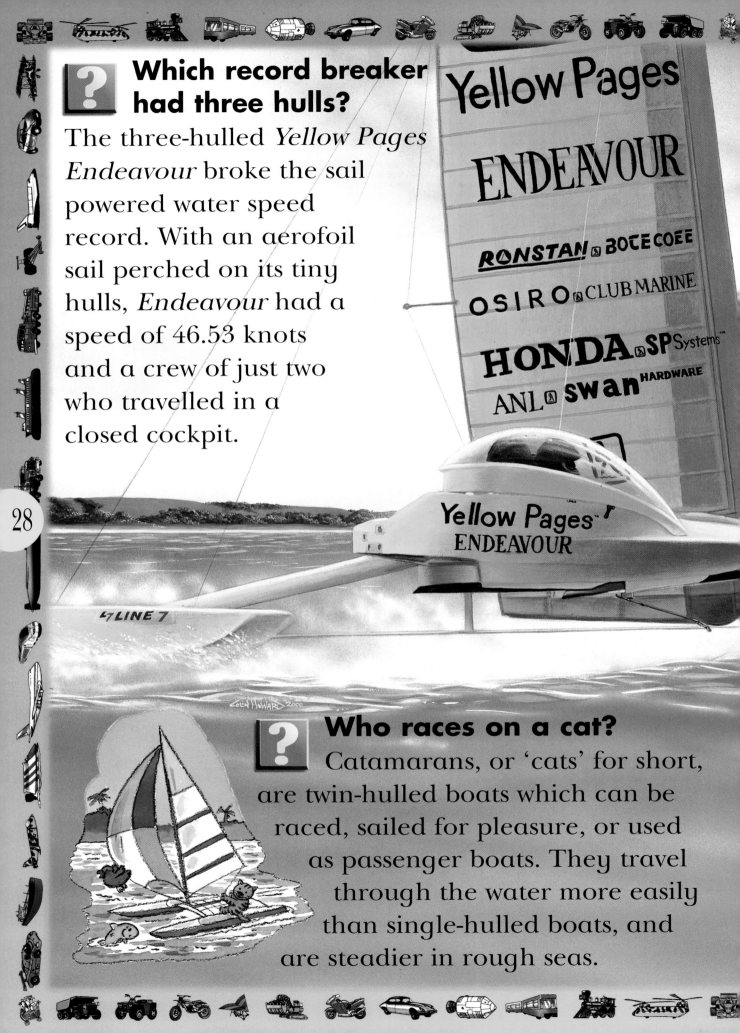

? Which record breaker had three hulls?

The three-hulled *Yellow Pages Endeavour* broke the sail powered water speed record. With an aerofoil sail perched on its tiny hulls, *Endeavour* had a speed of 46.53 knots and a crew of just two who travelled in a closed cockpit.

Yellow Pages
ENDEAVOUR

RONSTAN ⊡ BOTE COEE
OSIR O ⊡ CLUB MARINE
HONDA ⊡ SP Systems™
ANL ⊡ SWAN HARDWARE

Yellow Pages™
ENDEAVOUR

LINE 7

? Who races on a cat?

Catamarans, or 'cats' for short, are twin-hulled boats which can be raced, sailed for pleasure, or used as passenger boats. They travel through the water more easily than single-hulled boats, and are steadier in rough seas.

Sand yachts

Amazing! Some boats race all the way around the world, using only wind power. The Round The World Yacht Race is held every four years. Highly skilled sailors can even race 'the wrong way' around the world, against the wind and currents.

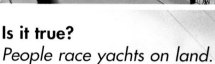
Is it true?
People race yachts on land.

Yes. Three wheeled sand yachts race along beaches at about 125 kph. Other yachts race along disused railway tracks, and even across snow!

29

Which boats skate on ice?

Iceboats can reach speeds of over 220 kph. They look like normal racing yachts, with tall sails and long ropes. But instead of hulls, they have skates which glide across the ice.

Iceboats

? What were Gee Bees?

American *Gee Bee* planes raced during the 1930s. The company which made them was called Granville Brothers (G.B.). These short, fat planes used to race at speeds of nearly 480 kph, in 8,800 kilometre-long races! Plane races were run to show how reliable the aircraft were.

30

MacRobertson race

? What was the longest air race?

The longest air race was the MacRobertson race from Mildenhall, England to Melbourne, Australia in 1934. It was won by the crew of a de Havilland in a time of 70 hours and 54 minutes.